Starting a Group Home Business

Copyright © 2024

All rights reserved. No part of this book may be reproduced in any form or by any electronic or mechanical means, including information storage and retrieval systems, without permission in writing from the publisher, except by a reviewer, who may quote brief passages in a review.

The information contained in this book is for general information purposes only. The information is provided by naciro and while we endeavor to keep the information up to date and correct, we make no representations or warranties of any kind, express or implied, about the completeness, accuracy, reliability, suitability or availability with respect to the book or the information, products, services, or related graphics contained in the book for any purpose. Any reliance you place on such information is therefore strictly at your own risk.

All trademarks and registered trademarks are the property of their respective owners and are used in this book only for identification and explanation.

Permission to use copyrighted material in this book should be obtained from the copyright owner or the publisher.

This book is not intended to provide medical, legal, or financial advice, and the author and publisher specifically disclaim any liability for any loss or damage caused or alleged to be caused directly or indirectly by the information in this book.

Naciro and the publisher of this book do not endorse or recommend any commercial products, processes, or services. The views and opinions of authors expressed in this book do not necessarily state or reflect those of the publisher of this book.

Table of Contents

1. Introduction to Group Homes
2. Understanding the Legal Requirements
3. Developing a Business Plan
4. Securing Funding and Resources
5. Finding the Right Location
6. Staffing Your Group Home
7. Developing Programs and Services
8. Marketing Your Group Home
9. Managing Day-to-Day Operations
10. Ensuring Compliance and Quality Standards
11. Building Community Relationships
12. Handling Emergencies and Crises
13. Financial Management and Budgeting
14. Evaluating and Improving Services
15. Future Trends and Expansion Opportunities

Introduction

Starting a group home business is a deeply rewarding endeavor that offers the opportunity to provide a supportive environment for individuals who need assistance in their daily lives. Whether you aim to serve the elderly, people with disabilities, or those with mental health issues, a group home can make a significant difference in your community. However, embarking on this journey requires careful planning, a thorough understanding of legal and regulatory requirements, and a strong commitment to creating a safe and nurturing environment for your residents.

In this comprehensive guide, we will walk you through every step of starting and running a successful group home business. From the initial planning stages to the day-to-day management of your facility, we will cover all aspects to ensure you are well-prepared to meet the needs of your residents and navigate the challenges of this industry.

The Importance of Group Homes

Group homes play a crucial role in providing care and support to individuals who cannot live independently. They offer a family-like setting where residents receive personalized care, emotional support, and opportunities for social interaction. These homes are essential for enhancing the quality of life for vulnerable populations and integrating them into the community.

Who Can Benefit from a Group Home?

Group homes cater to a variety of populations, including but not limited to:

- Elderly individuals who require assistance with daily living activities
- People with physical disabilities
- Individuals with developmental or intellectual disabilities
- Those recovering from mental health conditions
- Youths in foster care or transitioning out of juvenile detention

The Rewards of Running a Group Home

Operating a group home is not only a business opportunity but also a chance to make a meaningful impact. You will witness firsthand the positive changes in your residents' lives as they gain confidence, develop skills, and enjoy a higher quality of life. Additionally, running a group home can be financially rewarding, offering a stable income and the potential for growth as demand for such services increases.

Challenges to Consider

While the rewards are significant, running a group home comes with its own set of challenges. These include:

- Navigating complex legal and regulatory frameworks
- Securing adequate funding
- Managing a diverse team of caregivers
- Developing and maintaining high-quality programs and services
- Addressing the unique needs of each resident

Our Approach

This book is designed to be a practical guide, providing you with actionable steps and valuable insights from industry experts. Each chapter focuses on a critical aspect of starting and managing a group home, offering detailed information, tips, and best practices. By following this guide, you will be well-equipped to create a successful group home that makes a positive difference in your community.

Whether you are a seasoned healthcare professional looking to start your own group home or a newcomer to the industry with a passion for helping others, this guide will provide you with the knowledge and tools you need to achieve your goals. Let's embark on this rewarding journey together and create a brighter future for those in need.

Chapter 1: Introduction to Group Homes

Group homes are residential facilities designed to provide care and support to individuals who cannot live independently. These homes offer a family-like environment where residents receive personalized care and support tailored to their specific needs. The goal of a group home is to enhance the quality of life for its residents by promoting independence, social integration, and overall well-being.

Historical Context

The concept of group homes has evolved over time. Historically, individuals with disabilities or mental health issues were often placed in large institutions where they received minimal personal attention and care. These institutions were often overcrowded, underfunded, and operated under poor conditions. The deinstitutionalization movement of the mid-20th century marked a significant shift towards more humane and community-based care options.

In response to growing awareness of the need for better care, group homes emerged as an alternative to institutionalization. These smaller, community-based homes provide a more personalized and supportive environment, promoting the integration of residents into the community and enhancing their quality of life.

Types of Group Homes

Group homes can vary widely in terms of the populations they serve and the services they provide. Some common types of group homes include:

- **Elderly Care Homes**: These homes cater to seniors who require assistance with daily living activities, such as bathing, dressing,

and medication management. They provide a safe and supportive environment for elderly individuals who cannot live independently but do not require the intensive care of a nursing home.
- **Disability Support Homes**: These homes serve individuals with physical, developmental, or intellectual disabilities. They offer personalized care and support to help residents achieve greater independence and improve their quality of life.
- **Mental Health Group Homes**: These facilities provide a supportive environment for individuals recovering from mental health conditions. They offer therapeutic services, counseling, and support to help residents manage their conditions and integrate into the community.
- **Youth Group Homes**: These homes provide care and support to youths in foster care or those transitioning out of juvenile detention. They offer a stable and nurturing environment to help young people develop life skills and prepare for independent living.

Key Features of Group Homes

Regardless of the specific population they serve, all group homes share certain key features:

- **Personalized Care**: Group homes offer individualized care plans tailored to the unique needs of each resident. This ensures that residents receive the appropriate level of support and services to enhance their quality of life.
- **Community Integration**: Group homes promote the integration of residents into the community by providing opportunities for social interaction, recreational activities, and community involvement. This helps residents build relationships and develop a sense of belonging.

- **Safe and Supportive Environment**: Group homes provide a safe and supportive living environment where residents feel comfortable and secure. This includes ensuring that the physical environment is accessible and meets the needs of all residents.
- **Qualified Staff**: Group homes are staffed by qualified caregivers and support personnel who are trained to meet the specific needs of the residents. This includes providing medical care, therapeutic services, and emotional support.

The Role of Group Homes in the Community

Group homes play a vital role in the community by providing essential services to vulnerable populations. They offer a more humane and personalized alternative to institutional care, promoting the dignity and well-being of residents. Additionally, group homes contribute to the overall health and vitality of the community by creating jobs, supporting local businesses, and fostering a culture of inclusivity and support.

By understanding the importance and impact of group homes, we can better appreciate the value of starting and running such a facility. In the following chapters, we will delve into the practical aspects of establishing and managing a group home, providing you with the knowledge and tools you need to succeed in this rewarding endeavor.

Chapter 2: Understanding the Legal Requirements

Starting a group home involves navigating a complex web of legal and regulatory requirements. Ensuring compliance with these requirements is crucial for the successful operation of your facility and the well-being of your residents. In this chapter, we will explore the key legal considerations and steps you need to take to meet the necessary standards.

Licensing and Certification

One of the first steps in starting a group home is obtaining the necessary licenses and certifications. The requirements for licensing vary by state and locality, so it is important to research the specific regulations in your area. Generally, the licensing process involves submitting an application, undergoing inspections, and demonstrating that your facility meets certain standards of care and safety.

Key aspects of the licensing process include:

- **Application Process**: Completing and submitting the required application forms to the appropriate regulatory agency. This may involve providing detailed information about your facility, staffing, and services.
- **Inspections**: Undergoing inspections to ensure that your facility meets health, safety, and accessibility standards. This may include fire safety inspections, health department inspections, and building code inspections.
- **Staff Qualifications**: Demonstrating that your staff meets the required qualifications and training standards. This may involve background checks, certification requirements, and ongoing training.

Zoning and Building Codes

In addition to licensing requirements, you must also ensure that your facility complies with local zoning and building codes. Zoning regulations determine where group homes can be located and may impose specific requirements on the size, layout, and operation of the facility. Building codes set standards for the construction, maintenance, and safety of the physical environment.

Key considerations for zoning and building codes include:

- **Zoning Approval**: Obtaining zoning approval from your local zoning board or planning commission. This may involve submitting a site plan, attending public hearings, and addressing any concerns raised by the community.
- **Building Permits**: Securing the necessary building permits for any construction or renovation work. This ensures that your facility meets the required safety and accessibility standards.
- **Accessibility**: Ensuring that your facility is accessible to individuals with disabilities, in compliance with the Americans with Disabilities Act (ADA). This includes providing ramps, accessible bathrooms, and other necessary accommodations.

Health and Safety Regulations

Ensuring the health and safety of your residents is a top priority. This involves complying with a range of health and safety regulations, including those related to food safety, infection control, and emergency preparedness.

Key health and safety considerations include:

- **Food Safety**: Implementing food safety practices to prevent foodborne illnesses. This includes proper food storage, preparation, and handling procedures.
- **Infection Control**: Establishing infection control protocols to prevent the spread of infectious diseases. This may involve regular cleaning and disinfection, staff training, and vaccination policies.
- **Emergency Preparedness**: Developing and implementing an emergency preparedness plan to address potential emergencies such as fires, natural disasters, and medical emergencies. This

includes conducting regular drills and ensuring that staff and residents are familiar with emergency procedures.

Resident Rights and Protections

Protecting the rights and well-being of your residents is essential. This involves understanding and complying with regulations related to resident rights, privacy, and abuse prevention.

Key considerations for resident rights and protections include:

- **Resident Rights**: Ensuring that residents are aware of their rights and have access to information about their care and services. This includes respecting residents' autonomy, dignity, and privacy.
- **Privacy**: Implementing policies and procedures to protect residents' privacy and confidentiality. This includes safeguarding personal information and ensuring that residents' living spaces are private and secure.
- **Abuse Prevention**: Establishing policies and procedures to prevent and respond to abuse, neglect, and exploitation. This includes staff training, reporting protocols, and creating a culture of respect and accountability.

By understanding and complying with these legal requirements, you can ensure that your group home operates smoothly and provides a safe and supportive environment for your residents. In the next chapter, we will discuss the importance of developing a comprehensive business plan for your group home.

Chapter 3: Developing a Business Plan

A well-crafted business plan is the foundation of a successful group home. It serves as a roadmap for your business, outlining your goals, strategies, and financial projections. A comprehensive business plan not only helps you secure funding but also provides a clear framework for the growth and operation of your facility. In this chapter, we will explore the key components of a group home business plan and provide guidance on how to develop one.

Executive Summary

The executive summary is the first section of your business plan, but it is often written last. This section provides a brief overview of your business, highlighting the key points of your plan. It should be concise and compelling, capturing the essence of your group home and its mission.

Key elements of the executive summary include:

- **Mission Statement**: A clear and concise statement of your group's home's mission and purpose.
- **Business Objectives**: A summary of your short-term and long-term goals.
- **Key Services**: An overview of the services you will provide and the populations you will serve.
- **Financial Highlights**: A summary of your financial projections, including anticipated revenues, expenses, and profitability.

Market Analysis

A thorough market analysis is essential for understanding the demand for your services and identifying your target market. This section should include an analysis of the industry, the competitive landscape, and the needs of your target population.

Key components of the market analysis include:

- **Industry Overview**: An analysis of the group home industry, including trends, challenges, and opportunities.
- **Target Market**: A detailed description of the populations you will serve, including demographics, needs, and preferences.
- **Competitive Analysis**: An assessment of your competitors, including their strengths and weaknesses, and how you will differentiate your group home.
- **Market Needs**: An analysis of the unmet needs in your target market and how your group home will address them.

Organizational Structure

The organizational structure section outlines the management and staffing of your group home. This includes information about your leadership team, staff roles and responsibilities, and governance structure.

Key elements of the organizational structure include:

- **Management Team**: Profiles of your leadership team, including their qualifications, experience, and roles.
- **Staffing Plan**: An overview of your staffing needs, including the number and types of staff required, their qualifications, and their roles and responsibilities.
- **Organizational Chart**: A visual representation of your organizational structure, showing the relationships and reporting lines between different roles.

Services and Programs

The services and programs section provides a detailed description of the care and support services you will offer. This includes information about the types of services, the populations you will serve, and how you will deliver these services.

Key components of the services and programs section include:

- **Types of Services**: A description of the specific services you will provide, such as personal care, medical care, therapeutic services, and recreational activities.
- **Service Delivery Model**: An explanation of how you will deliver these services, including your approach to care, staffing, and scheduling.
- **Resident Programs**: Information about the programs and activities you will offer to enhance the quality of life for your residents, such as social events, educational programs, and community outings.

Marketing and Outreach

Effective marketing and outreach are essential for attracting residents and building relationships with referral sources. This section should outline your marketing strategies and tactics, as well as your approach to community outreach.

Key elements of the marketing and outreach section include:

- **Marketing Strategy**: An overview of your marketing goals and objectives, target audience, and key messages.

- **Marketing Tactics**: A description of the specific marketing tactics you will use, such as advertising, public relations, social media, and community events.
- **Outreach Plan**: An explanation of how you will build relationships with referral sources, such as healthcare providers, social workers, and community organizations.

Financial Plan

The financial plan is a critical component of your business plan, providing a detailed overview of your financial projections and funding needs. This section should include your revenue and expense projections, cash flow analysis, and funding requirements.

Key components of the financial plan include:

- **Revenue Projections**: An estimate of your anticipated revenues, including the sources of revenue (such as resident fees, government funding, and grants) and the assumptions underlying your projections.
- **Expense Projections**: An estimate of your anticipated expenses, including staff salaries, facility costs, program expenses, and administrative costs.
- **Cash Flow Analysis**: A projection of your cash flow, showing how much cash you expect to generate and spend each month.
- **Funding Requirements**: An explanation of your funding needs, including how much capital you need to start and operate your group home, and your plans for securing funding.

By developing a comprehensive business plan, you can ensure that your group home is well-positioned for success. This plan will serve as a valuable tool for guiding your decisions, attracting investors, and managing the growth and operation of your facility. In the next chapter, we will discuss strategies for securing funding and resources for your group home.

Chapter 4: Securing Funding and Resources

Starting a group home requires significant financial investment, and securing the necessary funding is often one of the biggest challenges entrepreneurs face. In this chapter, we will explore various funding options, provide tips for writing successful grant proposals, and discuss strategies for resource allocation to ensure your group home is financially sustainable.

Identifying Funding Sources

There are several potential funding sources for starting a group home, each with its own advantages and challenges. It's important to explore all available options and consider a diversified funding strategy to increase your chances of success.

1. Personal Savings and Loans

- **Personal Savings**: Using your own savings is the most straightforward way to fund your group home. This option gives you full control over your finances but also involves significant personal financial risk.
- **Loans**: You can obtain loans from banks, credit unions, or online lenders. It's important to compare interest rates, repayment terms, and eligibility requirements. A solid business plan can increase your chances of securing a loan.

2. Government Grants and Programs

- **Federal and State Grants**: Various government grants are available to support group homes, especially those serving vulnerable populations. Research programs offered by agencies like the U.S. Department of Health and Human Services (HHS) and the Administration for Community Living (ACL).
- **Local Government Programs**: Some local governments offer grants or low-interest loans to support community-based services. Contact your local government offices to learn about available programs.

3. Nonprofit Organizations and Foundations

- **Foundations**: Many foundations provide grants to support group homes and other social services. Research foundations that align with your mission and apply for relevant grants.
- **Nonprofit Organizations**: Partnering with established nonprofits can provide access to funding, resources, and expertise. Consider forming alliances with organizations that share your goals.

4. Community Fundraising and Donations

- **Fundraising Campaigns**: Launching a fundraising campaign can help you raise funds from your community. Use platforms like GoFundMe or Kickstarter to reach a broader audience.
- **Donations**: Seek donations from individuals, businesses, and community groups. Highlight the impact of your group home and the benefits it will bring to the community.

Writing Successful Grant Proposals

Securing grants is a competitive process, and writing a compelling grant proposal is crucial. Here are some tips to help you write effective grant proposals:

1. Understand the Requirements

- Carefully read the grant guidelines and ensure you meet all eligibility criteria. Follow the instructions precisely, including formatting and submission requirements.

2. Clearly Define Your Mission and Goals

- Clearly articulate your group's home's mission, objectives, and the specific needs you aim to address. Explain how your project aligns with the funding organization's goals.

3. Provide Detailed Plans and Budgets

- Outline your plans for implementing and managing the group home, including timelines, staffing, and program details. Provide a detailed budget that justifies your funding request and demonstrates how funds will be used effectively.

4. Highlight Your Expertise and Qualifications

- Showcase your team's expertise and experience in running similar programs or services. Provide evidence of your ability to manage the project successfully.

5. Demonstrate Community Support and Impact

- Provide letters of support from community organizations, local government officials, or other stakeholders. Highlight the positive impact your group home will have on the community and the specific populations you intend to serve.

6. Use Clear and Persuasive Language

- Write in a clear, concise, and persuasive manner. Avoid jargon and ensure your proposal is easy to understand. Use compelling narratives and real-life examples to illustrate the need for your group home and the difference it will make.

7. Include Evaluation and Sustainability Plans

- Detail how you will evaluate the success of your group home and measure its outcomes. Include plans for sustaining the group home beyond the grant period, showing your commitment to long-term success.

Strategies for Resource Allocation

Efficient resource allocation is crucial for the successful operation of your group home. Here are some strategies to help you manage your resources effectively:

1. Prioritize Essential Expenses

- Focus on allocating funds to essential expenses such as staff salaries, resident care, facility maintenance, and compliance with legal and safety standards. Ensure that your core operations are well-funded before allocating resources to other areas.

2. Implement Cost-Effective Practices

- Identify areas where you can reduce costs without compromising the quality of care. This may include bulk purchasing, negotiating discounts with suppliers, and using energy-efficient technologies to lower utility bills.

3. Leverage Community Resources

- Take advantage of community resources such as volunteer programs, donated goods, and partnerships with local businesses. Building strong community relationships can provide valuable support and reduce operational costs.

4. Regularly Review and Adjust Budgets

- Conduct regular reviews of your budget to monitor expenses and ensure you are staying within your financial plan. Adjust your budget as needed to address any unexpected costs or changes in funding.

5. Invest in Staff Training and Development

- Allocate resources for staff training and professional development. Well-trained staff can provide higher-quality care and are more likely to stay with your organization, reducing turnover and recruitment costs.

6. Develop a Contingency Plan

- Set aside funds for emergencies and unforeseen expenses. Having a contingency plan in place ensures that your group home can continue to operate smoothly in the face of unexpected challenges.

Chapter 5: Finding the Right Location

The location of your group home is critical to its success. Choosing the right location involves considering factors such as accessibility, safety, community resources, and regulatory requirements. In this chapter, we will discuss the key considerations for selecting a suitable location for your group home.

Assessing Accessibility and Convenience

Accessibility is a key factor in choosing a location for your group home. Consider the following aspects to ensure your residents, staff, and visitors can easily access your facility:

1. Proximity to Public Transportation

- Choose a location that is easily accessible by public transportation. This is particularly important for staff, visitors, and residents who may not have access to private vehicles.

2. Availability of Parking

- Ensure that there is adequate parking for staff, visitors, and service providers. Accessible parking spaces should be available for residents with disabilities.

3. Nearby Amenities and Services

- Select a location near essential amenities and services such as hospitals, medical clinics, grocery stores, pharmacies, and recreational facilities. Easy access to these services enhances the quality of life for your residents.

Evaluating Safety and Neighborhood Environment

The safety and environment of the neighborhood where your group home is located play a significant role in the well-being of your residents. Consider the following factors:

1. Crime Rates and Safety

- Research the crime rates in potential neighborhoods to ensure the safety of your residents. Choose a location with low crime rates and a strong sense of community safety.

2. Community Support and Engagement

- Evaluate the level of community support and engagement in potential neighborhoods. A supportive community can provide valuable resources, volunteer opportunities, and a welcoming environment for your residents.

3. Noise Levels and Environmental Factors

- Consider the noise levels and environmental factors such as air quality and green spaces. A peaceful and clean environment contributes to the overall well-being of your residents.

Understanding Zoning and Regulatory Requirements

Compliance with zoning laws and regulatory requirements is crucial when selecting a location for your group home. Consider the following aspects:

1. Zoning Laws and Permits

- Ensure that the location you choose complies with local zoning laws that allow for the operation of a group home. You may need to obtain special permits or variances, depending on the zoning regulations in the area.

2. Building Codes and Accessibility Standards

- Verify that the building meets all local building codes and accessibility standards, including those outlined by the Americans with Disabilities Act (ADA). This includes features such as ramps, wide doorways, and accessible bathrooms.

3. Health and Safety Inspections

- Ensure that the location passes all necessary health and safety inspections. This includes fire safety, sanitation, and overall building safety.

Securing the Property

Once you have identified a suitable location, the next step is to secure the property. This involves negotiating a lease or purchase agreement, conducting due diligence, and preparing the facility for operation.

1. Lease vs. Purchase

- Decide whether you will lease or purchase the property. Leasing may offer more flexibility and lower upfront costs, while purchasing can provide long-term stability and potential property appreciation.

2. Conducting Due Diligence

- Perform thorough due diligence to ensure the property is suitable for your needs. This includes a property inspection, reviewing the title and zoning status, and assessing any potential liabilities or restrictions.

3. Preparing the Facility

- Once you have secured the property, prepare the facility for operation. This may include renovations, furnishing, and ensuring compliance with all regulatory requirements. Create a timeline and budget for these preparations to ensure a smooth transition.

By carefully selecting the right location for your group home, you can create a safe, accessible, and supportive environment for your residents. In the next chapter, we will discuss the importance of staffing your group home and provide guidance on recruiting and retaining qualified personnel.

Chapter 6: Staffing Your Group Home

The success of your group home depends largely on the quality of your staff. Recruiting and retaining qualified, compassionate, and dedicated personnel is essential for providing high-quality care and creating a supportive environment for your residents. In this chapter, we will explore strategies for staffing your group home, including recruitment, training, and retention.

Identifying Staffing Needs

Before you begin the recruitment process, it's important to identify your staffing needs. Consider the following factors to determine the number and types of staff required for your group home:

1. Resident Needs

- Assess the specific needs of your residents, including their medical, personal care, and social support requirements. This will help you determine the types and levels of staffing needed to provide adequate care.

2. Staff Roles and Responsibilities

- Define the roles and responsibilities of each staff member. Common roles in a group home include caregivers, nurses, social workers, therapists, administrative staff, and support personnel.

3. Staffing Ratios

- Establish appropriate staffing ratios to ensure that residents receive adequate care and attention. Consider regulatory requirements and industry best practices when determining these ratios.

Recruitment Strategies

Recruiting qualified staff for your group home involves attracting candidates who possess the necessary skills, experience, and compassion for the job. Here are some effective recruitment strategies:

1. Job Postings and Advertising

- Post job openings on relevant job boards, websites, and social media platforms. Clearly outline the job requirements, responsibilities, and qualifications. Highlight the benefits of working at your group home, such as a supportive work environment and opportunities for professional development.

2. Networking and Referrals

- Leverage your professional network and seek referrals from trusted colleagues, partners, and community organizations. Personal referrals can often lead to high-quality candidates who are a good fit for your group home.

3. Job Fairs and Recruitment Events

- Participate in job fairs and recruitment events to connect with potential candidates. These events provide an opportunity to meet candidates in person, share information about your group home, and conduct preliminary interviews.

4. Collaboration with Educational Institutions

- Partner with local colleges, universities, and vocational schools that offer programs in healthcare, social work, and related fields. Establish internship or practicum opportunities to attract students and recent graduates.

Screening and Interviewing Candidates

Effective screening and interviewing processes are crucial for selecting the right candidates for your group home. Here are some tips for conducting thorough evaluations

1. Application Review

- Carefully review resumes and applications to identify candidates who meet the required qualifications and have relevant experience. Look for evidence of a commitment to caregiving and a genuine interest in working with your resident population.

2. Phone Screenings

- Conduct initial phone screenings to assess candidates' communication skills, availability, and basic qualifications. This helps narrow down the pool of candidates for in-person interviews.

3. In-Person Interviews

- Schedule in-person interviews with shortlisted candidates. Prepare a set of questions that assess their skills, experience, and suitability for the role. Include behavioral questions to evaluate how they handle various situations and challenges in a group home setting.

4. Reference Checks

- Contact the references provided by the candidates to verify their work history, performance, and suitability for the position. Ask specific questions related to their caregiving abilities, reliability, and interactions with residents.

5. Background Checks

- Conduct thorough background checks, including criminal history, employment verification, and professional license verification. Ensure that all candidates meet the legal and regulatory requirements for working in a group home.

Training and Development

Providing comprehensive training and development opportunities is essential for equipping your staff with the skills and knowledge they need to deliver high-quality care. Here are some key components of an effective training program:

1. Orientation and Onboarding

- Implement a structured orientation program to introduce new hires to your group home's policies, procedures, and culture. Provide an overview of their roles and responsibilities, and familiarize them with the facility and residents.

2. Mandatory Training

- Ensure that all staff complete mandatory training in areas such as CPR, first aid, infection control, medication administration, and emergency procedures. This training should be regularly updated to reflect current best practices and regulatory requirements.

3. Ongoing Education

- Offer ongoing education and training opportunities to help staff stay current with industry developments and enhance their skills. This may include workshops, seminars, online courses, and in-service training sessions.

4. Professional Development

- Support professional development by providing opportunities for staff to pursue certifications, advanced degrees, or specialized training. Encourage participation in professional organizations and conferences to promote networking and knowledge sharing.

Retention Strategies

Retaining qualified and dedicated staff is crucial for maintaining continuity of care and building a stable, supportive work environment. Here are some strategies to improve staff retention:

1. Competitive Compensation and Benefits

- Offer competitive salaries and benefits packages to attract and retain high-quality staff. Consider providing health insurance, retirement plans, paid time off, and other benefits that support staff well-being.

2. Positive Work Environment

- Foster a positive and supportive work environment where staff feel valued and respected. Encourage open communication, teamwork, and a culture of appreciation and recognition.

3. Work-Life Balance

- Promote work-life balance by offering flexible scheduling, part-time options, and support for staff dealing with personal or family challenges. Ensure that staff have adequate time off to rest and recharge.

4. Employee Recognition

- Implement an employee recognition program to acknowledge and reward staff for their hard work and dedication. This can include employee of the month awards, bonuses, public recognition, and other forms of appreciation.

5. Career Advancement Opportunities

- Provide clear pathways for career advancement within your group home. Offer promotions, leadership development programs, and opportunities for staff to take on new roles and responsibilities.

6. Feedback and Support

- Regularly seek feedback from staff about their job satisfaction, challenges, and suggestions for improvement. Provide support through regular check-ins, supervision, and access to resources such as counseling and stress management programs.

By implementing effective recruitment, training, and retention strategies, you can build a dedicated and skilled team that is committed to providing high-quality care for your residents. In the next chapter, we will discuss the importance of creating a supportive and engaging environment for your residents, focusing on individualized care plans and activities that enhance their quality of life.

Chapter 7: Creating a Supportive Environment for Residents

A supportive and engaging environment is essential for the well-being and quality of life of your residents. This chapter will explore strategies for developing individualized care plans, creating a positive living environment, and offering activities and programs that promote social interaction, mental stimulation, and overall wellness.

Developing Individualized Care Plans

Individualized care plans are crucial for meeting the unique needs of each resident. These plans should be comprehensive, person-centered, and regularly updated to reflect changes in the resident's health and preferences.

1. Initial Assessment

- Conduct a thorough initial assessment for each resident to understand their physical, emotional, and social needs. This assessment should include medical history, current health status, personal preferences, and any specific requirements.

2. Personalized Goals and Objectives

- Work with the resident, their family, and healthcare providers to set personalized goals and objectives. These goals should be realistic, measurable, and focused on enhancing the resident's quality of life.

3. Care Plan Development

- Develop a detailed care plan that outlines the services and support the resident will receive. This plan should include information on medical care, personal care, dietary needs, social activities, and any special accommodations.

4. Regular Reviews and Updates

- Schedule regular reviews of each care plan to ensure it remains relevant and effective. Update the plan as needed based on changes in the resident's condition, feedback from staff, and input from the resident and their family.

5. Collaborative Approach

- Foster a collaborative approach to care planning by involving the resident, their family, and a multidisciplinary team of healthcare providers. Encourage open communication and regular meetings to discuss progress and address any concerns.

Creating a Positive Living Environment

The physical and emotional environment of your group home plays a significant role in the well-being of your residents. Here are some strategies for creating a positive living environment:

1. Comfortable and Safe Facilities

- Ensure that your facility is comfortable, safe, and accessible. This includes maintaining clean and well-furnished living spaces, providing adequate lighting, and implementing safety features such as handrails and emergency call systems.

2. Personalization

- Allow residents to personalize their living spaces with their own belongings, such as photos, decorations, and furniture.

Personalization helps residents feel more at home and can enhance their sense of ownership and comfort.

3. Homelike Atmosphere

- Create a homelike atmosphere by incorporating elements such as cozy common areas, communal dining spaces, and outdoor areas for relaxation and recreation. Encourage residents to participate in household activities, such as gardening or decorating common areas.

4. Respect and Dignity

- Treat all residents with respect and dignity. Encourage staff to build positive relationships with residents, listen to their concerns, and provide support in a compassionate and respectful manner.

Offering Activities and Programs

Engaging activities and programs are essential for promoting social interaction, mental stimulation, and overall wellness. Here are some ideas for activities and programs that can enhance the quality of life for your residents:

1. Social Activities

- Organize regular social activities such as group outings, movie nights, game sessions, and holiday celebrations. These activities provide opportunities for residents to socialize, build friendships, and stay connected with the community.

2. Educational Programs

- Offer educational programs and workshops on topics of interest to your residents. This can include guest speakers, book clubs, arts and crafts classes, and computer literacy courses.

3. Physical Activities

- Encourage physical activity by providing opportunities for exercise and movement. This can include fitness classes, yoga sessions, walking groups, and recreational sports. Ensure that activities are accessible and suitable for residents of all abilities.

4. Therapeutic Activities

- Implement therapeutic activities such as music therapy, art therapy, and pet therapy to promote emotional well-being and relaxation. These activities can be particularly beneficial for residents with cognitive impairments or mental health challenges.

5. Volunteer and Community Involvement

- Facilitate opportunities for residents to volunteer and engage with the broader community. This can include organizing community service projects, participating in local events, or collaborating with community organizations.

6. Personalized Activities

- Offer personalized activities that cater to the individual interests and hobbies of your residents. This can include one-on-one sessions, small group activities, and special interest clubs.

7. Resident-Led Initiatives

- Encourage residents to take an active role in planning and leading activities. This empowers residents, fosters a sense of community, and ensures that activities align with their interests and preferences.

By developing individualized care plans, creating a positive living environment, and offering engaging activities and programs, you can enhance the quality of life for your residents and create a supportive, vibrant community. In the next chapter, we will discuss the importance of building strong relationships with residents' families and the wider community, and how to effectively communicate and collaborate with these stakeholders.

Chapter 8: Building Strong Relationships with Families and the Community

Strong relationships with residents' families and the wider community are essential for the success of your group home. Effective communication and collaboration with these stakeholders can enhance the support network for your residents, promote community involvement, and foster a positive reputation for your group home. In this chapter, we will explore strategies for building and maintaining these relationships.

Engaging with Residents' Families

Residents' families play a crucial role in their well-being and can provide valuable support and input. Here are some strategies for engaging with families:

1. Open and Honest Communication

- Maintain open and honest communication with residents' families. Provide regular updates on their loved one's well-being, care, and any changes in their condition. Be transparent about any challenges and involve families in decision-making processes.

2. Family Meetings

- Schedule regular family meetings to discuss care plans, address concerns, and provide information about upcoming events and activities. These meetings can also serve as a platform for families to provide feedback and suggestions.

3. Family Involvement in Care

- Encourage families to be actively involved in their loved one's care. This can include participating in care plan meetings, visiting regularly, and joining in activities and events.

4. Support Groups and Resources

- Offer support groups and resources for families to help them cope with the challenges of caregiving and navigate the healthcare system. This can include providing information on community resources, counseling services, and educational workshops.

5. Family Events and Activities

- Organize family events and activities to foster a sense of community and strengthen relationships. This can include holiday celebrations, family picnics, and special events where families can spend quality time with their loved ones.

Collaborating with the Community

Building strong connections with the wider community can enhance the resources and support available to your group home. Here are some strategies for community collaboration:

1. Community Partnerships

- Establish partnerships with local organizations, businesses, and healthcare providers to expand the services and support available to your residents. Collaborate on projects, share resources, and participate in community initiatives.

2. Volunteer Programs

- Develop a volunteer program to engage community members in supporting your group home. Volunteers can assist with activities, provide companionship to residents, and help with various tasks and events.

3. Community Outreach and Advocacy

- Participate in community outreach and advocacy efforts to raise awareness about the needs and contributions of your residents. This can include speaking at local events, participating in advocacy campaigns, and collaborating with other organizations to address common issues.

4. Public Relations and Marketing

- Promote your group home through public relations and marketing efforts. Highlight your successes, share positive stories, and engage with the media to build a positive reputation and attract support.

5. Open Houses and Tours

- Host open houses and tours to invite community members to visit your group home, learn about your services, and meet your residents and staff. This can help build relationships and foster a sense of community.

Managing Challenges and Conflicts

Building and maintaining relationships with families and the community can sometimes involve managing challenges and conflicts. Here are some strategies for addressing these issues effectively:

1. Conflict Resolution

- Develop a conflict resolution process to address disputes and concerns promptly and fairly. Encourage open communication, listen to all parties involved, and work collaboratively to find solutions.

2. Clear Policies and Procedures

- Establish clear policies and procedures for communication, visitation, and family involvement. Ensure that these policies are communicated to families and staff and are consistently applied.

3. Proactive Communication

- Be proactive in communicating with families and the community about any changes, challenges, or issues that may arise. Providing timely and accurate information can help prevent misunderstandings and build trust.

4. Feedback Mechanisms

- Implement feedback mechanisms, such as surveys or suggestion boxes, to gather input from families and the community. Use this feedback to make improvements and address any concerns.

By engaging with residents' families, collaborating with the community, and effectively managing challenges, you can build a strong support network for your group home. This not only enhances the well-being of your residents but also promotes a positive and inclusive environment. In the next chapter, we will discuss the importance of quality assurance and continuous improvement in maintaining high standards of care and service in your group home.

Chapter 9: Quality Assurance and Continuous Improvement

Maintaining high standards of care and service is essential for the success of your group home. Quality assurance and continuous improvement processes help ensure that your group home operates effectively, meets regulatory requirements, and provides the best possible care for your residents. In this chapter, we will explore strategies for implementing quality assurance and fostering a culture of continuous improvement.

Establishing Quality Assurance Processes

Quality assurance processes involve systematically monitoring, evaluating, and improving the quality of care and services provided in your group home. Here are some key components of an effective quality assurance program:

1. Setting Standards and Goals

- Establish clear standards and goals for the quality of care and services in your group home. These standards should align with regulatory requirements, industry best practices, and the needs and preferences of your residents.

2. Developing Policies and Procedures

- Create detailed policies and procedures that outline the standards for care, staff responsibilities, and operational practices. Ensure that these documents are comprehensive, easy to understand, and accessible to all staff members.

3. Monitoring and Evaluation

- Implement regular monitoring and evaluation processes to assess the quality of care and services. This can include conducting internal audits, reviewing resident care plans, and monitoring compliance with policies and procedures.

4. Resident and Family Feedback

- Regularly collect feedback from residents and their families to understand their experiences and identify areas for improvement. Use surveys, suggestion boxes, and face-to-face meetings to gather input.

5. Incident Reporting and Analysis

- Establish a system for reporting and analyzing incidents, such as accidents, medical errors, or complaints. Use this information to identify patterns, address root causes, and implement corrective actions.

Fostering a Culture of Continuous Improvement

Continuous improvement involves ongoing efforts to enhance the quality of care and services in your group home. Here are some strategies for fostering a culture of continuous improvement:

1. Staff Training and Development

- Provide regular training and development opportunities for your staff to ensure they have the skills and knowledge needed to deliver high-quality care. Encourage staff to stay current with industry best practices and advancements.

2. Empowering Staff

- Empower your staff to take an active role in quality improvement by encouraging them to identify issues and suggest solutions. Create an environment where staff feel valued and supported in their efforts to improve care.

3. Implementing Quality Improvement Projects

- Develop and implement quality improvement projects to address specific areas of concern or opportunities for enhancement. Use a structured approach, such as the Plan-Do-Study-Act (PDSA) cycle, to guide these projects.

4. Regular Team Meetings

- Hold regular team meetings to discuss quality assurance activities, review progress on improvement projects, and share best practices. Encourage open communication and collaboration among staff.

5. Celebrating Successes

- Recognize and celebrate the successes and achievements of your staff and residents in improving the quality of care. This can include formal awards, public recognition, and informal celebrations.

Utilizing Data and Technology

Leveraging data and technology can enhance your quality assurance and continuous improvement efforts. Here are some ways to incorporate data and technology into your processes:

1. Electronic Health Records (EHR)

- Implement an electronic health record (EHR) system to streamline the management of resident information, improve accuracy, and enhance communication among healthcare providers.

2. Data Analytics

- Use data analytics to track key performance indicators (KPIs) and identify trends and areas for improvement. Analyze data related to resident outcomes, staff performance, and operational efficiency.

3. Quality Management Software

- Consider using quality management software to support your quality assurance processes. These tools can help you track incidents, manage corrective actions, and monitor compliance with standards.

4. Telehealth and Remote Monitoring

- Utilize telehealth and remote monitoring technologies to enhance the care provided to residents. These tools can improve access to healthcare services, enable continuous monitoring, and support timely interventions.

Meeting Regulatory Requirements

Compliance with regulatory requirements is essential for the operation of your group home. Here are some strategies for ensuring compliance:

1. Staying Informed

- Stay informed about the regulatory requirements and standards that apply to your group home. This includes federal, state, and local regulations, as well as industry best practices.

2. Regular Audits and Inspections

- Conduct regular internal audits and inspections to assess compliance with regulatory requirements. Prepare for external inspections by regulatory agencies and address any identified issues promptly.

3. Documentation and Record-Keeping

- Maintain accurate and up-to-date documentation and records to demonstrate compliance with regulatory requirements. This includes resident records, staff training records, and incident reports.

4. Staff Training on Regulations

- Provide training for your staff on regulatory requirements and ensure they understand their responsibilities for compliance. Regularly update training to reflect any changes in regulations.

By implementing effective quality assurance processes, fostering a culture of continuous improvement, leveraging data and technology, and ensuring compliance with regulatory requirements, you can maintain high standards of care and service in your group home. In the next chapter, we will explore the financial management aspects of running a group home, including budgeting, financial planning, and strategies for sustainability.

Chapter 10: Financial Management and Sustainability

Effective financial management is critical to the success and sustainability of your group home. This chapter will cover key aspects of financial management, including budgeting, financial planning, revenue generation, and strategies for ensuring long-term sustainability.

Budgeting and Financial Planning

Creating and managing a budget is essential for controlling costs and ensuring the financial stability of your group home. Here are some steps for effective budgeting and financial planning:

1. Establishing a Budget

- Develop a detailed budget that outlines all projected income and expenses for your group home. Include categories such as staff salaries, utilities, food, medical supplies, maintenance, and administrative costs.

2. Monitoring Expenses

- Regularly monitor and track your expenses to ensure you stay within your budget. Use accounting software or financial management tools to help you keep accurate records and identify any discrepancies.

3. Adjusting the Budget

- Periodically review and adjust your budget based on actual income and expenses. Make necessary adjustments to address any shortfalls or unexpected costs.

4. Financial Forecasting

- Conduct financial forecasting to predict future financial performance and identify potential challenges. Use historical data and trends to inform your forecasts and plan for different scenarios.

Revenue Generation

Generating sufficient revenue is crucial for covering your operating costs and funding improvements. Here are some strategies for increasing revenue:

1. Diversifying Funding Sources

- Diversify your funding sources to reduce dependence on a single source of income. Explore options such as government grants, private donations, fundraising events, and partnerships with local businesses.

2. Maximizing Occupancy Rates

- Aim to maximize the occupancy rates of your group home by actively marketing your services and maintaining a positive reputation in the community. Ensure that your facility is always ready to accommodate new residents.

3. Fee Structures

- Review and adjust your fee structures to ensure they are competitive and reflect the quality of care and services you provide. Consider offering tiered pricing or additional services for an extra fee.

4. Grants and Fundraising

- Apply for grants from government agencies, foundations, and other organizations that support group homes and community services. Organize fundraising events and campaigns to raise additional funds.

Cost Control and Efficiency

Controlling costs and improving efficiency are essential for maintaining financial health. Here are some strategies for cost control and efficiency:

1. Cost-Benefit Analysis

- Conduct cost-benefit analyses for major expenses and investments to ensure they provide value for money. Evaluate the potential benefits and costs of new initiatives or improvements before proceeding.

2. Energy Efficiency

- Implement energy-efficient practices to reduce utility costs. This can include using energy-efficient appliances, installing LED lighting, and optimizing heating and cooling systems.

3. Bulk Purchasing

- Purchase supplies in bulk to take advantage of discounts and reduce per-unit costs. Establish relationships with suppliers to negotiate better prices and terms.

4. Streamlining Operations

- Streamline your operations to eliminate waste and improve efficiency. This can include optimizing staff schedules, improving workflow processes, and using technology to automate tasks.

Financial Reporting and Accountability

Maintaining transparency and accountability in financial management is essential for building trust with stakeholders and ensuring the long-term sustainability of your group home. Here are some key practices:

1. Regular Financial Reporting

- Prepare regular financial reports to provide an overview of your group home's financial performance. Share these reports with your board of directors, staff, and other stakeholders as appropriate.

2. Audits and Reviews

- Conduct regular internal and external audits to ensure the accuracy and integrity of your financial records. Address any findings or recommendations from audits promptly.

3. Accountability Measures

- Implement accountability measures to ensure responsible financial management. This can include setting spending limits, requiring multiple approvals for large expenses, and maintaining clear records of all financial transactions.

4. Transparency with Stakeholders

- Maintain transparency with your stakeholders about your group's home's financial status and any financial challenges.

Communicate openly about your financial strategies and any changes that may impact residents or services.

By practicing effective financial management, generating sufficient revenue, controlling costs, and maintaining transparency and accountability, you can ensure the financial sustainability of your group home. In the final chapter, we will summarize the key steps and considerations for successfully operating a group home and provide additional resources for ongoing support and development.

Chapter 11: Summary and Additional Resources

Operating a successful group home requires careful planning, effective management, and a commitment to providing high-quality care. This chapter will summarize the key steps and considerations discussed throughout this guide and provide additional resources for ongoing support and development.

Key Steps and Considerations

1. Developing a Vision and Mission

- Clearly define the vision and mission of your group home to guide your planning and operations.

2. Legal and Regulatory Compliance

- Understand and comply with all legal and regulatory requirements for operating a group home, including licensing, zoning, and health and safety standards.

3. Securing Funding and Resources

- Explore various funding options, including personal savings, loans, grants, and community fundraising. Develop a comprehensive funding strategy to ensure financial stability.

4. Finding the Right Location

- Choose a location that is accessible, safe, and meets zoning and regulatory requirements. Ensure the facility is comfortable and suitable for your residents' needs.

5. Staffing Your Group Home

- Recruit, train, and retain qualified staff who are committed to providing high-quality care. Foster a positive work environment and support ongoing professional development.

6. Creating a Supportive Environment for Residents

- Develop individualized care plans, create a positive living environment, and offer engaging activities and programs to enhance residents' quality of life.

7. Building Strong Relationships with Families and the Community

- Engage with residents' families, collaborate with the community, and manage challenges and conflicts effectively.

8. Implementing Quality Assurance and Continuous Improvement

- Establish quality assurance processes, foster a culture of continuous improvement, and leverage data and technology to enhance care and services.

9. Managing Finances and Ensuring Sustainability

- Practice effective financial management, generate sufficient revenue, control costs, and maintain transparency and accountability.

Additional Resources

To support your ongoing development and success, consider utilizing the following resources:

1. Professional Organizations

- Join professional organizations related to group home management and caregiving, such as the National Association of Residential Care Facilities (NARCF) or the National Council for Community Behavioral Healthcare (NCCBH). These organizations offer networking opportunities, training, and advocacy support.

2. Training and Education

- Pursue continuing education and training opportunities for yourself and your staff. Look for workshops, online courses, and certification programs that cover topics such as caregiving, management, and regulatory compliance.

3. Regulatory Agencies

- Stay informed about regulations and guidelines by regularly visiting the websites of relevant regulatory agencies, such as the Department of Health and Human Services (HHS) and the Centers for Medicare & Medicaid Services (CMS).

4. Community Resources

- Utilize community resources such as local health departments, social service agencies, and nonprofit organizations. These resources can provide support, funding, and services that benefit your group home and residents.

5. Online Forums and Support Groups

- Participate in online forums and support groups for group home operators and caregivers. These platforms can offer valuable advice, peer support, and information on best practices.

By following the steps and strategies outlined in this guide and leveraging available resources, you can successfully operate a group home that provides high-quality care and enhances the lives of your residents. Remember to stay committed to continuous improvement, engage with your community, and prioritize the well-being of your residents.

Conclusion

Running a group home is a challenging yet rewarding endeavor that requires dedication, compassion, and effective management. By developing a clear vision, ensuring compliance, securing funding, staffing appropriately, creating a supportive environment, building strong relationships, implementing quality assurance, managing finances, and utilizing available resources, you can create a thriving group home that provides exceptional care and support to your residents.

Thank you for your commitment to improving the lives of those in need. Your efforts make a significant difference in the well-being and quality of life of your residents, and your dedication to excellence sets a positive example for others in the field.

Chapter 12: Marketing and Outreach Strategies

Successfully running a group home not only requires excellent internal management but also effective marketing and outreach to attract residents and gain community support. In this chapter, we will explore strategies for marketing your group home, building your brand, and engaging with the community to ensure sustained occupancy and a positive reputation.

Developing a Marketing Plan

A well-thought-out marketing plan is essential for reaching potential residents and their families. Here are key components to include in your marketing plan:

1. Identifying Your Target Audience

- Define your target audience, which typically includes potential residents, their families, healthcare professionals, and social service agencies. Understanding their needs and preferences will help tailor your marketing efforts.

2. Setting Marketing Objectives

- Establish clear marketing objectives, such as increasing inquiries, boosting occupancy rates, or enhancing community awareness. These objectives should be specific, measurable, attainable, relevant, and time-bound (SMART).

3. Budgeting for Marketing

- Allocate a budget for your marketing activities. Consider costs for advertising, promotional materials, events, and digital marketing efforts. Ensure that your budget aligns with your overall financial plan.

4. Choosing Marketing Channels

- Identify the most effective marketing channels for reaching your target audience. This may include online platforms, print media, community events, and partnerships with local organizations.

Building Your Brand

Creating a strong and recognizable brand is crucial for differentiating your group home from others and building trust with potential residents and their families. Here are steps to build and strengthen your brand:

1. Crafting Your Brand Identity

- Develop a clear and consistent brand identity, including your group home's name, logo, colors, and tagline. Your brand identity should reflect your mission, values, and the unique aspects of your services.

2. Creating a Compelling Message

- Craft a compelling message that communicates the benefits of your group home. Highlight what sets your home apart, such as personalized care, a supportive community, or specialized services.

3. Building an Online Presence

- Create a professional website that provides detailed information about your group home, including services offered, staff qualifications, testimonials, and contact information. Ensure your website is user-friendly and optimized for search engines (SEO).

4. Leveraging Social Media

- Use social media platforms like Facebook, Instagram, and LinkedIn to engage with your audience, share updates, and showcase the daily life and activities in your group home. Social media can also be a powerful tool for receiving feedback and interacting with the community.

Engaging with the Community

Community engagement is vital for building relationships, gaining referrals, and enhancing your group's home's reputation. Here are some strategies for effective community engagement:

1. Hosting Open Houses and Tours

- Regularly host open houses and tours to invite potential residents, families, and community members to visit your group home. These events provide an opportunity to showcase your facilities and services and build personal connections.

2. Participating in Community Events

- Take part in local events, such as health fairs, festivals, and charity fundraisers. Setting up a booth or sponsoring an event can increase visibility and demonstrate your commitment to the community.

3. Building Partnerships

- Develop partnerships with local healthcare providers, social service agencies, and community organizations. These partnerships can lead to referrals, collaborative projects, and additional resources for your group home.

4. Offering Educational Workshops

- Host educational workshops and seminars on topics related to caregiving, health, and wellness. These events can position your group home as a knowledgeable and valuable resource in the community.

Effective Communication

Clear and consistent communication is essential for marketing and outreach. Here are some tips for effective communication with your target audience:

1. Creating Informative Materials

- Develop informative materials, such as brochures, flyers, and newsletters, that provide detailed information about your group home and its services. Distribute these materials at community events, healthcare facilities, and online.

2. Personalizing Outreach Efforts

- Personalize your outreach efforts by addressing potential residents and their families by name and tailoring your messages to their specific needs and concerns. Personal touches can make a significant impact.

3. Utilizing Testimonials and Reviews

- Collect and share testimonials and reviews from current residents and their families. Positive feedback can build credibility and trust with potential residents and their families.

4. Implementing Follow-Up Processes

- Establish follow-up processes for inquiries and visits. Promptly respond to questions, provide additional information, and maintain contact with potential residents and their families.

By developing a comprehensive marketing plan, building a strong brand, engaging with the community, and communicating effectively, you can attract residents, gain community support, and ensure the long-term success of your group home. In the next chapter, we will explore strategies for managing crises and emergencies, ensuring the safety and well-being of your residents and staff.

Chapter 13: Managing Crises and Emergencies

Crisis management and emergency preparedness are critical aspects of operating a group home. Ensuring the safety and well-being of your residents and staff during crises requires thorough planning, training, and effective response strategies. In this chapter, we will discuss how to prepare for and manage various types of emergencies, from natural disasters to health crises.

Developing an Emergency Preparedness Plan

An emergency preparedness plan outlines the procedures and resources needed to respond effectively to emergencies. Here are key steps to develop a comprehensive plan:

1. Identifying Potential Emergencies

- Identify the types of emergencies that could affect your group home, such as natural disasters (e.g., hurricanes, earthquakes, floods), health crises (e.g., pandemics, outbreaks), and other emergencies (e.g., fire, power outages).

2. Creating Emergency Procedures

- Develop detailed procedures for each type of emergency. These procedures should include steps for evacuation, shelter-in-place, communication, and coordination with emergency services.

3. Assigning Roles and Responsibilities

- Assign specific roles and responsibilities to staff members for various aspects of emergency response. Ensure that all staff are aware of their duties and trained to perform them effectively.

4. Establishing Communication Protocols

- Establish clear communication protocols for notifying residents, staff, families, and emergency services during an emergency. Include multiple methods of communication, such as phone calls, text messages, and public announcements.

Training and Drills

Regular training and drills are essential for ensuring that your staff and residents are prepared to respond to emergencies. Here are some strategies for effective training and drills:

1. Staff Training

- Provide comprehensive training for staff on emergency procedures, including evacuation routes, first aid, CPR, and the use of emergency equipment. Update training regularly to reflect any changes in procedures or new threats.

2. Resident Education

- Educate residents on emergency procedures and what to expect during different types of emergencies. Conduct regular information sessions and provide written materials that are easy to understand.

3. Conducting Drills

- Schedule regular drills for various types of emergencies, such as fire drills, earthquake drills, and lockdown drills. Use these drills to practice procedures, identify areas for improvement, and ensure everyone is familiar with their roles.

4. Evaluating and Improving

- After each drill, evaluate the effectiveness of the response and identify any issues or areas for improvement. Update your emergency preparedness plan and training programs based on these evaluations.

Ensuring Safety During Health Crises

Health crises, such as pandemics and infectious disease outbreaks, pose unique challenges for group homes. Here are some strategies for managing health crises:

1. Infection Control Measures

- Implement strict infection control measures, including regular handwashing, use of personal protective equipment (PPE), cleaning and disinfecting protocols, and isolation of affected individuals.

2. Monitoring and Reporting

- Monitor residents and staff for signs of illness and establish protocols for reporting and managing suspected cases. Work closely with local health authorities to ensure timely reporting and response.

3. Communication with Families

- Maintain open and transparent communication with residents' families about the health crisis, the measures being taken to protect residents, and any changes in policies or procedures.

4. Supporting Mental Health

- Provide support for the mental health and well-being of residents and staff during health crises. Offer counseling services, virtual activities, and other resources to help manage stress and anxiety.

Coordinating with Emergency Services

Collaboration with local emergency services is essential for effective crisis management. Here are some tips for coordinating with emergency services:

1. Building Relationships

- Establish relationships with local emergency services, including fire departments, police, and emergency medical services. Participate in community emergency planning and response initiatives.

2. Sharing Information

- Share your emergency preparedness plan with local emergency services and ensure they are familiar with your facility and its specific needs. Provide them with contact information and key details about your residents and staff.

3. Coordinating Response Efforts

- During an emergency, coordinate closely with emergency services to ensure a timely and effective response. Follow their guidance and support their efforts to protect your residents and staff.

By developing a comprehensive emergency preparedness plan, providing regular training and drills, implementing infection control measures, and coordinating with emergency services, you can ensure the safety and well-being of your residents and staff during crises. In the next chapter, we will explore strategies for fostering a positive work environment and supporting your staff's professional development and well-being.

Chapter 14: Fostering a Positive Work Environment

Creating a positive work environment is essential for retaining qualified staff, enhancing their job satisfaction, and ensuring high-quality care for your residents. This chapter will discuss strategies for fostering a supportive, inclusive, and engaging work environment that promotes professional development and well-being.

Building a Supportive Culture

A supportive culture is the foundation of a positive work environment. Here are some strategies to build a supportive culture:

1. Open Communication

- Foster open communication by encouraging staff to share their ideas, concerns, and feedback. Hold regular meetings and create channels for anonymous feedback to ensure everyone feels heard.

2. Recognizing and Rewarding Staff

- Recognize and reward staff for their hard work and dedication. Implement a recognition program that highlights achievements and milestones, and consider offering incentives such as bonuses, gift cards, or additional time off.

3. Providing Support Resources

- Offer resources to support staff well-being, such as counseling services, stress management workshops, and wellness programs. Show your commitment to their physical and mental health.

4. Encouraging Teamwork

- Promote teamwork by organizing team-building activities, encouraging collaboration, and fostering a sense of camaraderie among staff members. A strong team dynamic can improve morale and job satisfaction.

Professional Development and Growth

Supporting your staff's professional development and growth is key to retaining talent and ensuring high-quality care. Here are some strategies for fostering professional development:

1. Offering Training and Education

- Provide ongoing training and education opportunities to help staff enhance their skills and stay current with industry best practices. Offer workshops, online courses, and certification programs relevant to their roles.

2. Career Advancement Opportunities

- Create clear pathways for career advancement within your group home. Encourage staff to pursue leadership roles and provide mentorship and support to help them achieve their career goals.

3. Performance Evaluations

- Conduct regular performance evaluations to provide constructive feedback and identify areas for growth. Use evaluations as an opportunity to discuss career aspirations and create development plans.

4. Supporting Continuing Education

- Support staff in pursuing continuing education by offering tuition reimbursement, flexible scheduling, and time off for coursework. Investing in their education benefits both the staff and the group home.

Creating a Safe and Inclusive Workplace

A safe and inclusive workplace is essential for the well-being and satisfaction of your staff. Here are some strategies to create a safe and inclusive environment:

1. Promoting Diversity and Inclusion

- Promote diversity and inclusion by implementing policies that ensure equal opportunities for all staff, regardless of their background. Encourage a culture of respect and inclusivity.

2. Addressing Workplace Harassment

- Establish clear policies for preventing and addressing workplace harassment. Provide training on recognizing and reporting harassment, and ensure that all complaints are taken seriously and addressed promptly.

3. Ensuring Workplace Safety

- Maintain a safe work environment by adhering to health and safety regulations, conducting regular safety inspections, and providing safety training for staff. Ensure that all staff are aware of emergency procedures and have access to necessary safety equipment.

4. Supporting Work-Life Balance

- Support work-life balance by offering flexible scheduling, paid time off, and policies that accommodate personal needs. Recognize the importance of staff having time to recharge and spend with their families.

By building a supportive culture, investing in professional development, creating a safe and inclusive workplace, and supporting work-life balance, you can foster a positive work environment that attracts and retains talented staff. In the final chapter, we will provide a comprehensive summary and additional resources to support your continued success in operating a group home.

Chapter 15: Final Thoughts and Ongoing Support

As you embark on the journey of operating a group home, it is essential to remain committed to continuous improvement, community engagement, and the well-being of your residents and staff. This final chapter will provide a comprehensive summary of the key steps and considerations discussed throughout this guide, as well as additional resources for ongoing support and development.

Comprehensive Summary

1. Developing a Vision and Mission

- Establish a clear vision and mission to guide your group's home's planning and operations.

2. Legal and Regulatory Compliance

- Ensure compliance with all legal and regulatory requirements, including licensing, zoning, and health and safety standards.

3. Securing Funding and Resources

- Explore diverse funding options and develop a comprehensive funding strategy for financial stability.

4. Finding the Right Location

- Choose a suitable location that meets zoning and regulatory requirements and is accessible and safe.

5. Staffing Your Group Home

- Recruit, train, and retain qualified staff, fostering a positive work environment and supporting professional development.

6. Creating a Supportive Environment for Residents

- Develop individualized care plans, offer engaging activities, and create a positive living environment.

7. Building Strong Relationships with Families and the Community

- Engage with residents' families, collaborate with the community, and manage challenges effectively.

8. Implementing Quality Assurance and Continuous Improvement

- Establish quality assurance processes, foster a culture of continuous improvement, and leverage data and technology.

9. Managing Finances and Ensuring Sustainability

- Practice effective financial management, generate sufficient revenue, control costs, and maintain transparency.

10. Marketing and Outreach Strategies

- Develop a comprehensive marketing plan, build a strong brand, engage with the community, and communicate effectively.

11. Managing Crises and Emergencies

- Prepare for and manage various types of emergencies, ensuring the safety and well-being of residents and staff.

12. Fostering a Positive Work Environment

- Create a supportive, inclusive, and engaging work environment that promotes professional development and well-being.

Additional Resources

To support your ongoing success, consider utilizing the following resources:

1. Professional Organizations

- Join organizations such as the National Association of Residential Care Facilities (NARCF) or the National Council for Community Behavioral Healthcare (NCCBH) for networking, training, and advocacy support.

2. Training and Education

- Pursue continuing education and training opportunities for yourself and your staff, including workshops, online courses, and certification programs.

3. Regulatory Agencies

- Regularly visit the websites of regulatory agencies like the Department of Health and Human Services (HHS) and the Centers for Medicare & Medicaid Services (CMS) for updates on regulations and guidelines.

4. Community Resources

- Utilize local health departments, social service agencies, and nonprofit organizations for support, funding, and services that benefit your group home and residents.

5. Online Forums and Support Groups

- Participate in online forums and support groups for group home operators and caregivers to gain valuable advice, peer support, and information on best practices.

By following the steps and strategies outlined in this guide and leveraging available resources, you can successfully operate a group home that provides high-quality care and enhances the lives of your residents. Stay committed to continuous improvement, engage with your community, and prioritize the well-being of your residents and staff. Your dedication to excellence makes a significant difference in the well-being and quality of life of those you serve.

Thank you for your commitment to improving the lives of those in need. Your efforts make a meaningful impact, and your dedication to creating a supportive and caring environment sets a positive example for others in the field.

Conclusion: Wishing You Success

Congratulations on reaching the conclusion of this comprehensive guide to starting and operating a group home. The journey you are embarking on is both challenging and incredibly rewarding, offering you the opportunity to make a significant difference in the lives of those in need. As you implement the strategies and insights shared in this book, you are well on your way to creating a thriving, compassionate, and effective group home.

The key to your success lies in your dedication to continuous improvement, your ability to adapt to changing circumstances, and your unwavering commitment to the well-being of your residents and staff. By developing a clear vision and mission, ensuring legal and regulatory compliance, securing funding, finding the right location, and building a strong team, you lay a solid foundation for your group home. Creating a supportive environment for your residents, engaging with the community, implementing quality assurance processes, and managing finances effectively will help you sustain and grow your group home over time.

Your efforts to foster a positive work environment, invest in professional development, and maintain open communication with residents' families and the community will further enhance the quality of care you provide. Preparing for and managing crises, along with implementing robust marketing and outreach strategies, ensures that your group home remains a safe, welcoming, and well-regarded institution.

As you move forward, remember that your dedication, compassion, and commitment to excellence set a positive example for others in the field. You are not only providing a vital service but also contributing to the well-being and quality of life of your residents, their families, and the broader community.

Thank you for your commitment to this important work. Your efforts are deeply appreciated and have a lasting impact on the lives of those you serve. Wishing you all the best in your endeavors, and may your group home thrive and continue to provide exceptional care and support for many years to come.

With all my best wishes for your success

www.ingramcontent.com/pod-product-compliance
Lightning Source LLC
Chambersburg PA
CBHW072053230526
45479CB00010B/930